A Note to Parents

Dorling Kindersley Classic Readers is a compelling new program for beginning readers, designed in conjunction with leading literacy experts, including Dr. Linda Gambrell, President of the National Reading Conference and past board member of the International Reading Association.

Beautiful illustrations and superb full-color photographs combine with engaging, easy-to-read stories to offer a fresh approach to each subject in the series. Each *Dorling Kindersley Classic Reader* is guaranteed to capture a child's interest while developing his or her reading skills, general knowledge, and love of reading.

The four levels of *Dorling Kindersley Classic Readers* are aimed at different reading abilities, enabling you to choose the books that are exactly right for your children:

Level 1, for **Preschool to Grade 1**
Level 2, for **Grades 1 to 3**
Level 3, for **Grades 2 and 3**
Level 4, for **Grades 2 to 4**

The "normal" age at which a child begins to read can be anywhere from three to eight years old, so these levels are intended only as a general guideline.

No matter which level you select, you can be sure that you are helping your child learn to read, then read to learn!

A Dorling Kindersley Book
www.dk.com

Created by Leapfrog Press Ltd

Project Editor Naia Bray-Moffatt
Art Editor Catherine Goldsmith

For Dorling Kindersley
Senior Editor Marie Greenwood
Managing Art Editor Jacquie Gulliver
Managing Editor Joanna Devereux
Production Chris Avgherinos
Picture Researcher Liz Moore
Cover Design Margherita Gianni

Reading Consultant
Linda B. Gambrell, Ph.D.

First American edition, 2000
2 4 6 8 10 9 7 5 3 1

Published in the United States by Dorling Kindersley
Publishing, Inc.
95 Madison Avenue, New York, New York 10016

Dorling Kindersley Classic Readers™ is a trademark
of Dorling Kindersley Limited, London.

A catalog record is available from the Library of Congress.

ISBN 0-7894-5391-6

The publisher would like to thank the following for their kind
permission to reproduce their photographs:
Key: t=top, a=above, b=below, c=centre
AKG London: 4t, 34t, 40t; Art & Ancient Architecture: 6t; 13t, 27b, 29t; Graham
Black, Nottingham Trent University: 46t, 47crl; Bridgeman Art Library: 16t, cl, 17b,
18b, 22t. 23t, 26t, 27t, 32t, 37t, 38b, 39t, 41t; Jean Loup Charmet: 44b; Christie's
Images: 13b; ET Archive: 12b, 28t, 32b, 33b, 40b,;Mary Evans Picture Library: 4b, 14t,
34b, 36b, 43b, 44t; Ronald Grant Archive: 25b, 35t; Sonia Halliday Photographs: 42t;
Robert Harding Picture Library: 18t, 22b; Kobal Collection 5b;
Nottingham Museum & Art Gallery: 5t.
Additional photography by: London Dungeon/Norman Hollands, Museum of London,
Nottingham County Council, Jane Thompson, Wallace Collection.

Color reproduction by Colourscan, Singapore
Printed and bound in Belgium by Proost

Contents

Man or myth?   4

Robert of Huntingdon   6

Mysterious Robin Hood   8

Maid Marian joins
the outlaws   22

Sir Richard of Lee   26

Archery adventure   30

Long live the king!   36

Bad times return   40

The last arrow   46

Glossary   48

Level
4
GRADES 2-4

ROBIN HOOD

THE TALE OF THE GREAT OUTLAW HERO

By Angela Bull
Illustrated by Nick Harris

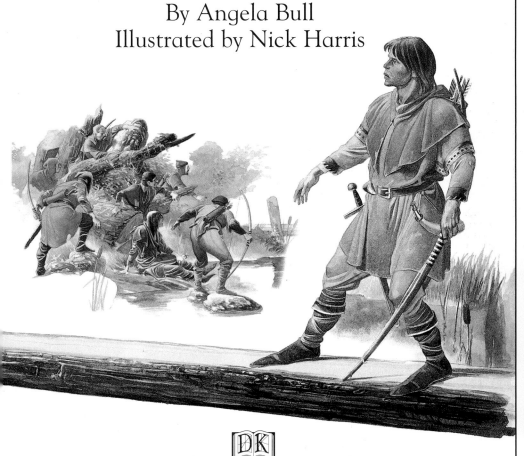

Dorling Kindersley
www.dk.com

Robin the hero
Robin Hood's legend inspired many stories and pictures from early days. This woodcut dates from about 1600.

Outlaws
An outlaw was someone put outside the protection of the law. They often went to live in forests, where no one could find them.

Man or myth?

Everyone has heard of Robin Hood, the medieval English outlaw, who robbed the rich to give to the poor. But was he a real person?

The earliest mention of Robin Hood comes in a Yorkshire document of 1230, which describes in Latin, "Robertus Hood, fugitivus" (Robin Hood, outlaw). This was followed by many songs and stories about the outlaw Robin Hood, which were finally collected in 1795 by a writer called Joseph Ritson.

After studying them, Ritson felt able to state firmly that Robin Hood was a real person. He was born at Locksley in Nottinghamshire in 1160, his name was Robert Fitzooth, and he was believed to be the Earl of Huntingdon.

Whatever the true facts of his life, Robin Hood has been loved and admired for centuries.

The stories about this hero have a special mixture of action and good causes. There are daring deeds and great fights as well as loyalty to the true king and to the poor and needy. They have inspired books, movies, and television programs; and the places associated with Robin have become favorite tourist attractions.

This book tells just a few of the many stories about the outlaw and his band of Merry Men.

Attraction
Tourists flock to look at this bronze statue of Robin Hood in Nottingham.

From the 1991 TV program Robin Hood and his Merry Men

Robert of Huntingdon

All of England was in turmoil. The king, Richard the Lionheart, had gone abroad to fight. Richard's brother, Prince John, ruled in his place. His subjects hated and feared him.

One fine spring morning Robert Fitzooth, Earl of Huntingdon, had forgotten his country's troubles. He was walking in Sherwood Forest with Marian Fitzwalter, the girl he loved. She looked so beautiful that Robert went down on one knee.

"Marian, I love you. Will you marry me?" he asked.

"Oh yes!" replied Marian. "I will. I love you, too."

The next moment they were in each other's arms. Neither of them noticed that they were not alone. They were overheard by Worman, a spy working for John's wicked ally, the Sheriff of Nottingham.

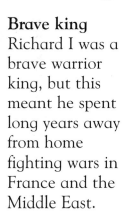

Brave king
Richard I was a brave warrior king, but this meant he spent long years away from home fighting wars in France and the Middle East.

Sheriff
Sheriffs were powerful men. They collected taxes and carried out the king's justice.

7

Mysterious Robin Hood

Nottingham Castle
The Sheriff of Nottingham lived in the castle, which was on a small hill overlooking the town.

The Sheriff frowned when Worman told him the news. "I don't want to hear anything good about my enemy," he growled.

Following Prince John's orders, the Sheriff robbed and ill-treated the poor around Nottingham. Only Robert Fitzooth was brave enough to stand up to him.

"Wait a minute," said Worman. "Have you heard of the man in Sherwood Forest who is the people's hero?

The leader of a daring band of outlaws who rob the rich, then give the money to the poor?"

"Yes," snapped the Sheriff. "It's the man they call Robin Hood. I don't know who he is, but I know that I hate him."

Worman dropped his voice.

"Robin Hood is another name for Robert Fitzooth," he whispered. "I was his servant once, and I know for certain."

"Thank you!" said the Sheriff. "You've done well. Prince John and I want Robin Hood tossed in jail. We will catch him at his wedding. Here, take this."

He tossed Worman a purse of gold coins.

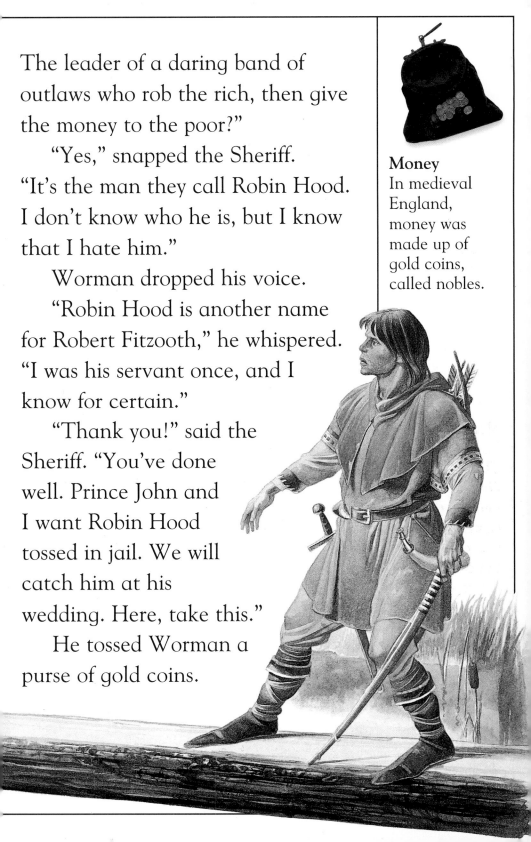

Money
In medieval England, money was made up of gold coins, called nobles.

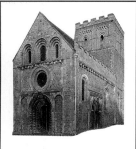

Norman church
The wedding was probably in a Norman style church. These buildings were normally cross-shaped, with a square tower and rounded arches.

A crowd filled the church for the wedding of Robert Fitzooth and Marian Fitzwalter. As the priest began the service, a troop of armed men burst in, led by the Sheriff. With him was Sir Guy of Gisborne, another friend of Prince John's.

"Stop the wedding!" shouted the Sheriff. "The Earl of Huntingdon is a traitor." Robert spun around.

"That's not true," he exclaimed. "I am loyal to the king."

"King Richard has left England," sneered the Sheriff. "It's Prince John who rules now, and he has declared you an outlaw. You must forfeit your lands and title. Anyone who kills you will be rewarded with five shillings."

Well dressed
Wealthy brides such as Marian wore elaborate headdresses. Their dresses were long with wide sleeves, and were not always white.

Sherwood Forest
This was one of the largest forests in the country, covering about 19,000 acres (7,800 hectares).

Armed men closed in, but Robert drew his sword and slashed a path through them.

At the door he paused. "Wait for me, Marian!" he cried. "I'll be in Sherwood Forest." Then, mounting his horse, he galloped off before anyone could stop him.

Sir Guy eyed Marian. Could he marry her himself, he wondered.

11

Sherwood
Sherwood was a royal forest – reserved by the king for hunting deer and boar. Prince John loved to go hunting there.

Major Oak
Robin Hood is thought to have camped by this oak tree in Sherwood Forest. It is one of the oldest trees in England.

Now Robert was an outlaw like the others in his band. He'd led them into action many times before, but had then gone back to his manor house, Locksley Hall. After John's condemnation, he settled down in Sherwood Forest with his band of Merry Men, and openly called himself Robin Hood.

They made hideouts for safety in the densest woodland and made suits of Lincoln green clothes for camouflage. They practiced archery every day and held many shooting competitions. Robin was the best shot of them all.

The outlaws hunted the royal deer to eat at their feasts. This was a crime, but they didn't care. They would ask Richard's pardon when he returned. Meanwhile, they declared war on John's supporters, who had become rich by taxing the poor.

The outlaws ambushed wealthy travelers on the forest road. They treated them well and gave them venison for dinner, before removing their purses and other valuable items. The money went straight to poor people, who loved the outlaws and supported Richard, the rightful king.

Travelers in danger
The forest was well known as a place where travelers might be ambushed.

Stories flew around Nottingham about the outlaws under Robin's command. One of the best was about how Little John joined the band.

Robin was walking alone in Sherwood Forest one day, wearing his usual Lincoln green, when he came to a stream spanned by a narrow plank bridge. Just as Robin stepped onto one end of the bridge, a second man stepped onto the other.

He was a giant-sized fellow with massive arms and legs.

"Look out, little man!" he shouted out to Robin. "Let me cross."

"Wait a minute," Robin replied. "It's my right of way."

Close combat
Arguments were often settled by hand-to-hand fighting instead of by more peaceful methods.

Lincoln Green
Robin Hood and his Merry Men wore cloth of a dull green color, called Lincoln green. It was cheap to buy and good camouflage.

"Nonsense. Clear off, or I'll duck you in the water," threatened the tall stranger. Speedily, Robin put an arrow to his bow. Any more threats, and he'd shoot.

"Coward!" taunted the tall man. "I've no bow, so it's not a fair fight. But I have got my quarterstaff." He brandished an enormous stick.

"Find one for yourself, and we'll fight it out."

"Right!" agreed Robin quickly.

He plunged into the forest and hacked down a six-foot branch.

"I'll get you now!" he shouted.

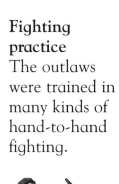

Robin sprang back onto the bridge and aimed a blow at the big man. Bang, crash, went the quarterstaffs. The two men fought on, trying not to slip on the narrow plank. Robin leaped forward to attack again, and the stranger knocked him into the water. Then the giant knelt down and held out his stick for Robin to grasp. Robin pulled himself up, dripping wet, as his men rushed out of the forest.

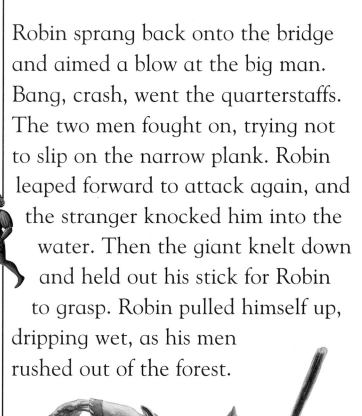

"Robin! Are you hurt?" they called. Robin wasn't often beaten.

"No. It was a fair fight," said Robin, "and this man won."

"What is your name?" asked one of the outlaws.

"I'm called John Little," replied the stranger.

"You should be called Little John!" joked Robin, looking at his size. "And I am Robin Hood."

"I was looking for you," smiled Little John. "I want to join the outlaws and fight for King Richard!"

Little John
In real life, there was a John Little who came from a small village in Barnsdale Forest, north of Sherwood Forest.

Water warriors
Water-tilting involved knocking tilters off opposing boats. This was particularly popular among young men.

Fountains Abbey
The ruins of the abbey where Friar Tuck stayed in Yorkshire still stand today.

Friars
Friars were religious men who wandered from place to place teaching about the life of Christ.

Many tales were told about the adventures of Robin Hood and Little John. They were both great archers and strong fighters. But people sometimes spoke of a man who was even stronger – Brother Michael Tuck, a friar at Fountains Abbey. One day Robin, with six outlaws, set off to find him.

Soon they found a friar sitting by a river. He was so fat, he was nearly round. He had a sword in his belt.

Telling the outlaws to hide, Robin strolled down to the water.

"Will you carry me across the river?" he asked the friar. The friar heaved Robin onto his back and strode across.

"Thanks!" Robin jumped down, but the friar drew his sword. "Wait a moment," he snapped. "I want to get back to my side. Now it's your turn to carry me."

Robin stumbled through the water with the friar on his back. He was exhausted when he reached the bank but he managed to draw his sword.

"Now, carry me back again," he demanded.

The friar lifted Robin onto his back and waded into the river. Halfway across he jerked his shoulders. Robin splashed headlong into the icy water.

"Sink or swim," he cried. "I'll not carry you one step further."

Struggling out, Robin fired an arrow. The friar laughed and caught the arrow with his shield. In a fury Robin rushed at him and they clashed swords.

Medieval sword
These large, heavy swords were swung with both hands.

Hunting horn
Horns were used for signaling on a hunt or in battle. They were usually made from hollowed-out cattle horns. When blown they made a deep sound that carried through the thickest forest.

Hunting dog
Fierce dogs, such as this mastiff, were used to hunt wolves and were also pitted to fight against one another.

Very soon, Robin realized that fat Friar Tuck was too strong for him. He blew his horn and six outlaws charged out of the bushes to help him.

The friar only grinned. He gave a loud whistle and a pack of hunting dogs raced up. Their sharp teeth fastened in the outlaws' clothes – Robin saw that they had no chance. Besides, he liked the fierce, fat friar.

"Stop!" he shouted. "Let's not fight. I am Robin Hood. Will you join my Merry Men? We live in the forest, roast the king's deer and help the poor by taking from the rich."

"That sounds good enough for me," said Friar Tuck, laughing, "especially the roast venison. I will serve you and your outlaw band as priest for as long as you reign in the forest."

So Friar Tuck joined Robin's Merry Men and proved to be as loyal and brave as any of the outlaws.

Fighting clergy
From 1417 until 1429, a priest named Robert Stafford led a band of outlaws. He called himself "Friar Tuck" after the legendary friar.

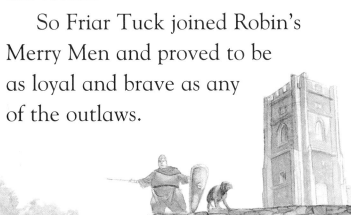

Women's work
While waiting for Robin to return, Marian would have spent her days learning wifely duties. These included weaving.

Manor house
Noblemen lived in manor houses, which had strong walls for defense.

Maid Marian joins the outlaws

The strength and popularity of the outlaws infuriated Prince John and the Sheriff, and they racked their brains for a way of punishing them. Then the Sheriff had an idea. He summoned Sir Guy of Gisborne.

"If you can capture Robin Hood," he told Sir Guy, "you can have his lands and his bride."

Marian was horrified when Sir Guy appeared at her father's house.

"Marry you? Never," she cried. "I will only marry Robert Fitzooth."

"I'll stay here till he comes to see you. Then I'll get him," threatened Sir Guy. He tried to kiss her, but Marian flinched away.

"Never mind. When Robin's caught, you'll be my wife," vowed Sir Guy. Marian hurried to her room.

She dressed quickly in a page's clothes, which she had hidden in a cupboard. Disguised as a pageboy, she slipped out of the side gate of the manor house. Then she ran off along a secret path between the trees to Robin's forest hideaway.

Pageboys
Boys who were going to be knights trained as pageboys. They learned to serve knights and ladies.

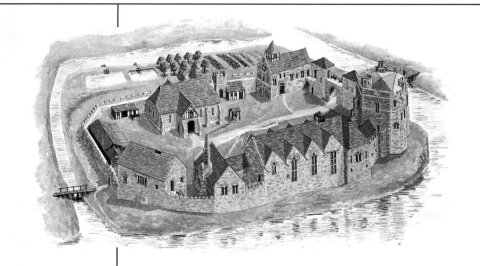

In disguise
As she was slim, Marian was easily able to disguise herself in a young boy's clothing.

The next morning Prince John and the Sheriff arrived at Marian's father's manor house.

"We've come to witness the wedding of Sir Guy and your daughter Marian," they announced. "Bring her here."

The servants hurried to fetch Marian, but her room was empty. They searched the whole manor house, and still they couldn't find her.

Prince John summoned the guard from the side gate.

"Did anyone leave here last night?" he demanded.

"Only a young pageboy, sir," answered the guard.

"That was Marian! She's tricked us," cried Sir Guy.

Sir Guy, Prince John, and the Sheriff were left fuming helplessly, for by then Marian was far away. Knowing the forest paths, she reached the hideout next evening.

"I want to join Robin Hood," she told an outlaw.

Robin Hood climbed down from a tree. "No, boy, you're far too young," he said.

"Don't you recognize me?" cried Marian.

She pulled off her page's cap and the next moment she was in Robin's arms. "But I will not marry you," she told him, "until King Richard comes home."

Film version Robin, played by Errol Flynn, and Marian in the 1938 movie, *The Adventures of Robin Hood.*

Sir Richard of Lee

Roasting
At outdoor feasts, deer meat, called venison, was roasted on a long spit over a charcoal fire.

Knight
In medieval times, knights were warriors who followed a code of good behavior, called chivalry.

Robin Hood had killed a large stag. As it roasted over the fire, he looked at the outlaws. "We need a guest at this feast. Find a rich traveler who'll pay for his dinner," he suggested.

Little John and two others waited by the main road through Sherwood Forest. Soon they saw a knight approaching on horseback.

26

"He doesn't look very rich," muttered Little John, eyeing the knight's tattered clothing. "But he might do."

Politely he invited the knight to share Robin's venison.

The knight, Sir Richard of Lee, accepted. Although he ate hungrily, he looked miserable.

Robin asked why.

"My son was captured with King Richard," the knight explained. "To raise money for his ransom, I borrowed four hundred pounds from the Abbot of St. Mary's. I should repay him today but I've no money left. He'll take my lands instead and I will have no home."

The Abbot was a cruel friend of Prince John's.

"I won't allow that!" Robin exclaimed. "Here's four hundred pounds. Pay your debt and return the money to me next year."

Smart knights
Knights did not always wear shining armor. Some, like Sir Richard, fell on hard times.

Abbot
Rich abbots often loaned money to landowners, who had to give up their estates if they failed to repay on time.

Cellarer
The cellarer of an abbey was in charge of the wine used in services and at meals. The wine was usually kept in cellars.

Locked up
Even kings and noble prisoners were kept locked in handcuffs until their family paid a ransom for their release.

A year later, the Merry Men were waiting for Sir Richard when two monks rode into the forest. "More guests! Join our feast," the outlaws invited.

As the monks sat down to plates of roast venison, Robin Hood asked them where they were from.

"St. Mary's Abbey," one monk replied. "I am the Abbot, and this is the cellarer."

Robin raised an eyebrow. "Then you must be rich."

"No. We've got nothing," the Abbot protested.

Little John opened their bags and found eight hundred pounds in gold coins hidden there.

"This must be payment for your dinner," he remarked.

"That money is for Prince John!" the monks screeched together.

"He already has too much," said Little John, pleased to take it.

When they had ridden angrily away, Sir Richard arrived to repay his four hundred pounds.

Robin wouldn't take it.

"Keep your money. The Abbot of St. Mary's has paid instead," he explained. "Have you got your son back? And is there any news of our lost king?"

"My son is safe," said Sir Richard. "But no one has ransomed the king."

"Prince John doesn't want him home," sighed Robin. "Will he ever return?"

Durnstein Castle
King Richard was imprisoned at this castle in Germany on his way back from fighting in the Middle East.

Clay jug
Potters made
their goods at
home, then sold
them at local
town markets.

Archery adventure

One day, determined to catch
Robin, the Sheriff planned a way of
luring the outlaw out of the forest.
He announced an archery contest,
with a silver arrow as the prize.

When Robin heard about it,
he longed to take part. He waited
by a forest trail until a potter came
along, driving a cart. Robin stopped
the man and persuaded him to
exchange clothes.

Cleverly disguised, Robin drove into Nottingham and began selling pots at the archery ground.

When the last archer had shot his arrow, Robin stepped forward and asked for a turn. Raising his bow, he hit the middle of the target.

"So a worthless potter has won," grumbled the Sheriff, handing Robin the prize. "Let me see his arrow."

Someone brought it over.

"It's made with peacock feathers!" the Sheriff exclaimed. "Robin Hood uses peacock feathers! Catch that potter! He must be Robin Hood in disguise."

But the Sheriff's men were too slow. Laughing, and waving the silver arrow, Robin drove back to Sherwood.

Archery contest
Archery was a popular sport in Robin Hood's day, and competitions were common.

Prize arrows
Most arrows were trimmed with cheap goose feathers. Peacock feathers were rare and expensive.

Butcher
Butchers bought farm animals to kill and then sell at market.

Market
Once a week, traders came into market towns like Nottingham, and the rich townsfolk went shopping.

The disguise plan had worked so well, and it was such fun tricking the Sheriff, that Robin decided to try it again. This time he changed clothes with a butcher and, after a safe journey along busy roads, he set up a meat stall in the middle of Nottingham market.

It wasn't long before the Sheriff's wife came past and Robin offered her a free joint of meat. She was so delighted with the gesture that she invited Robin to have dinner with the Sheriff.

Robin was amused to find himself sitting by the Sheriff at table.

When the Sheriff inquired if he sold horned beasts (meaning cattle) Robin tried a trick.

"Certainly," he said. "I've got two hundred horned beasts for sale, and a hundred acres of land as well. Are you interested?"

"Very interested," said the Sheriff. "I'd pay three hundred pounds for the lot."

"It's a deal," Robin soon replied. "And if you ride home with me after dinner, I can show you the beasts. But bring the money with you."

As soon as dinner was over, the Sheriff called for his horse to be saddled. He didn't think of bringing any guards or servants. He was only taking a short ride with a harmless butcher.

He and Robin headed for Sherwood Forest.

"Be careful," warned the Sheriff. "Robin Hood might attack us!"

Horned beast
Today, cows' horns are removed for safety. In medieval times, cows could have very long horns.

Noble horse
Noblemen such as the Sheriff rode well-bred, fast horses called palfreys:

Forest deer
In the last few hundred years, forests have been chopped down to make way for farms and cities. The number of wild deer has fallen dramatically.

Poaching
Poachers, who hunted illegally, faced terrible punishments if brought before the strict forest courts.

"Don't worry," answered Robin. "Look!" He pointed to a herd of deer. "Here are some of my horned beasts. How do you like them?"

"The deer in this forest belong to Prince John," snapped the Sheriff. "Poaching them may be punished by death. And where are your hundred acres?"

"All around us. I am Robin Hood and all Sherwood Forest belongs to me!" Robin blew his horn. Several outlaws sprang from the bushes and surrounded the Sheriff. "Bind his eyes and bring him to our camp for supper," Robin ordered.

Blindfolded, the terrified Sheriff was led to Robin's secret hideout. Roast venison and wine stolen from his own cellar was offered to him, while Little John removed the money from his pockets.

"Let us keep his fine horse, too," Robin suggested.

At last, Robin led the Sheriff back to Nottingham and removed the blindfold.

"You will pay for this!" the Sheriff threatened. "I will catch you in the end!"

But Robin only chuckled and vanished back into the dark forest.

Robin Hood
Robin laughs as he leaves his victims poorer, but wiser.

35

Long live the king!

Exciting rumors spread through Sherwood Forest. People said that King Richard had returned. Prince John and the Sheriff fumed. Could it be true?

One day, the outlaws found a tall pilgrim traveling in the forest. They invited him to a dinner of roast venison. Robin noticed how keenly he watched them from under the brim of his hat.

"Why do you live outdoors like this?" the pilgrim suddenly asked.

"Prince John drove us from our homes," they answered.

The pilgrim sighed deeply. To cheer him up, Robin suggested a shooting match.

He said that the pilgrim could knock down any outlaw who missed the target!

It was Robin himself who missed – distracted by a fluttering bird.

Pilgrims
These were men and women who traveled across Europe to visit holy shrines.

"Hit me!" he said, laughing and looking straight up under the pilgrim's hat. All at once, he dropped down to his knees.

"Is it really you, King Richard?" he gasped.

"Arise, Robert, Earl of Huntingdon," said the king. "I have heard about your loyalty to me and your generosity to the poor. I hereby pardon you of any crimes and restore your lands and title."

Archery
Targets were usually set up on earthen mounds, called butts. Anything might be used as a target.

Robin bowed his grateful thanks and immediately summoned his priest, Friar Tuck.

"Now that the king is home," he said, "you can marry me and Maid Marian."

The friar read the wedding service and the king gave Robin and Marian his blessing. He told all the outlaws that they were pardoned for the crimes they had committed. There was feasting and rejoicing in Sherwood Forest.

The next day King Richard rode in state into Nottingham. Robin Hood, who could once again be called Robert Fitzooth, rode beside him. The crowds in Nottingham went wild with joy. Prince John and the Sheriff just had time to grab their horses and escape.

Robin and Marian went
to live at Robin's old home,
Locksley Hall, with friends
including Little John and
Friar Tuck. The other outlaws
joined the king's army.

And everywhere in
England tales and ballads about
Robin Hood and his Merry Men
were told and sung.

That should have been the
happy ending to the story.
But it wasn't.

Richard I dies
King Richard died in 1199. He was hit by a crossbow bolt while besieging the castle of Chalus in France. His grave can be seen in France.

Richard I

Crossbow

Bad times return

King Richard didn't stay long in England. He was a determined warrior and he was soon off to fight a war in France. He pardoned Prince John for his wicked actions, but John wasn't sorry.

After five years came dreadful news. King Richard had been killed; and as he had no son, John became the lawful king. With his old crony, the Sheriff of Nottingham, he was soon plotting revenge on Richard's supporters. He summoned Sir Guy of Gisborne and asked for his help in trapping Robert Fitzooth.

"Go to Sherwood Forest," John advised. "He has probably returned there."

Sir Guy disguised himself under a horse's skin and, taking his sword, went to wait in the forest. He didn't have to wait long.

Robin and Little John soon came past, talking anxiously. They were worried about friends whom Richard could no longer protect. When they saw the man in the horse skin, they both halted.

"Who are you? What are you doing here?" Robin asked.

"Hunting," replied the man.

"What animals?" Robin asked.

"None. I'm hunting Robin Hood."

Robin recognized his old enemy, Sir Guy, beneath the horse's mane. "I am Robin!" he cried, and instantly drew his sword.

King John
King Richard's brother, Prince John, was crowned in May 1199. Nicknamed "Bad King John," his policies led to widespread discontent.

41

Mummer
Dancers, called mummers, wore horse costumes. They were a symbol of courage and protection.

Sir Guy pushed back the horse's head and whipped out his sword. In a moment, he and Robin were fighting hard. Both men were good fighters and the battle swayed to and fro across a forest clearing. Suddenly Robin tripped over a tree root. As he stumbled, Sir Guy thrust his sword into Robin's side with a cry.

Wounded, and hardly knowing what he was doing, Robin struck with his own weapon. It pierced Sir Guy's neck and he fell to the ground, dead.

Little John had been watching in horror. Now he ran over and caught Robin as he fainted from his wound.

"This looks serious," Little John muttered. "I must get him home."

He carefully carried Robin back to Locksley Hall, where Marian put him to bed.

Even her thankfulness that Sir Guy was dead did not ease Marian's worries about her husband. It was many weeks before Robin was able to get up again.

Clearing
Open spaces were common in forests. In a process called coppicing, groups of trees would be cut back to the stumps for timber, and left to regrow.

Bedchamber
Only the rich had private bedrooms with actual beds to lie on. Most people slept on the floor.

When Robin had partly recovered, he decided to go to church in Nottingham. A spy noticed him there and hurried to the Sheriff with the news.

Immediately the Sheriff sent men to arrest him. So at last, with his hands manacled, Robin was dragged before his old enemy.

The Sheriff chuckled with glee. "Lock him in the deepest dungeon!" he commanded.

Marian despaired when the news reached Locksley Hall but Friar Tuck took control.

Hurrying toward Nottingham, he met a messenger carrying a letter from King John that told the Sheriff to have Robin executed.

"I'm going that way. I'll take the letter for you, if you like," the friar offered kindly, and the messenger handed it over.

"I've brought you a letter from the king," Friar Tuck told the Sheriff. "And I've orders to see the prisoner myself."

The Sheriff sent a jailer to show him the dungeon. The friar quickly overpowered him, locked him in a cell and set Robin free.

The trial of Robin was due to begin the next morning. The Sheriff arrived with grim satisfaction. But there was no prisoner in the dungeon. The Sheriff had been tricked again!

Dungeons
Dungeons were normally in castle cellars. The jailer was paid a fee to guard each prisoner.

The last arrow

Kirklees Priory
This priory was founded by Henry II, the father of King Richard.

Marian had already fled to Kirklees Priory. It seemed right for Friar Tuck and Little John to take Robin there too, as the Prioress was his cousin. They did not know that the Prioress's father had hated Robin's father for inheriting Locksley Hall, and that she herself was full of spite toward Robin.

When Robin was put to bed, the Prioress sent everyone out of the room. Telling Robin that it would help him, she cut open a vein in his arm.

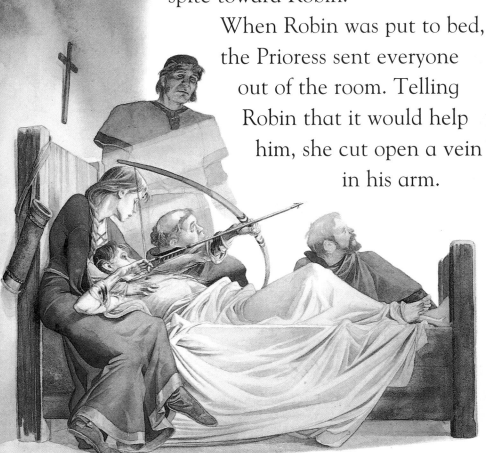

As the blood flowed, Robin felt dizzy and weak. Somehow he grasped his horn and blew a feeble note. Immediately Marian, Little John, and Friar Tuck came to him.

"I am dying," murmured Robin. "Give me my bow."

Before his strength failed him, Robin shot his last arrow through the window, out into the forest.

"Bury me where the arrow has fallen," he whispered.

A moment later, he died in Marian's arms. The outlaws found the arrow and, in that woodland spot, with great sorrow, they buried the hero, Robin Hood.

Here, underneath this little stone
Lies Robert, Earl of Huntingdon
No archer was as he so good
And people called him Robin Hood
Such outlaws as he and his men
Will England never see again

Robin's grave
Legend has it that this gravestone at Kirklees is Robin's. There is nothing written on the stone. The verse in the story was found among the Dean of York's papers in 1700.

Glossary

Abbot
The person who is in charge of the monks in an abbey.

Archery
The sport of shooting with bows and arrows.

Ballad
A song that tells a story, often with a chorus.

Camouflage
Dressing, painting, or covering something to look like the landscape it is found in.

Cellarer
The monk responsible for the food and drink in an abbey.

Condemn
To declare someone guilty and give them a punishment.

Earl
An English nobleman. In medieval times, an earl would be the owner of a large part of a kingdom.

Forfeit
To give something up as a punishment for making a mistake or committing a crime.

Friar
A member of a religious order in the Roman Catholic Church. Friars were usually preachers who wandered from place to place.

Legend
A story that is based on true events and people. Legends are handed down from generation to generation through storytelling and singing, and now books and TV.

Lincoln green
Strong cloth of a dull green color that was hard-wearing and cheap to buy, like blue denim is now.

Loyalty
Being faithful to one's country, king, family, or beliefs.

Medieval
Belonging to the period of European history between about 500 and 1450.

Monk
A man living and working in a Christian or other religious community.

Outlaw
A person who has committed a crime and no longer has the protection of the law.

Pageboy
A boy in training for knighthood who worked for a knight.

Pilgrim
A person who goes on a journey to a holy place in their religion, as an act of religious duty.

Poaching
Breaking the law by hunting animals on someone's private property.

Priory
The home of a group of nuns governed by a prioress.

Quarterstaff
A thick wooden staff, sometimes tipped with iron, about 3 feet long. Quarterstaffs were used as weapons in medieval England.

Ransom
The amount of money that must be paid in order that a prisoner be released.

Sheriff
An officer of the king who collected taxes and could act as a judge.

Shilling
A coin worth one-twentieth of a British pound. No more shillings were made in Britain after 1970.

Venison
The flesh of a deer, which is eaten as food, usually roasted.